Grandmother's

NOTES

Canadian representatives: General Publishing Co., Ltd.,
30 Lesmill Road, Don Mills, Ontario M3B 2T6.

9 8 7 6 5 4 3 2 1
Digit on the right indicates the number of this printing.

ISBN 1–56138–581–6

Cover design by Toby Schmidt
Interior design by Frances J. Soo Ping Chow
Cover and interior illustrations by Valerie Coursen
Edited by Tara Ann McFadden
Typography by Justin T. Scott
Printed in the United States

This book may be ordered by mail from the publisher.
Please add $1.00 for postage and handling.
But try your bookstore first!

Running Press Book Publishers
125 South Twenty-second Street
Philadelphia, Pennsylvania 19103–4399

Grandmother's
NOTES

RUNNING PRESS
PHILADELPHIA · LONDON

A child is born only once,

while a grandparent is reborn with each new grandchild.

Arthur Kornhaber
20th-century American writer

$\mathcal{G}$randchildren provide us with some of our proudest occasions, some of our tenderest experiences, and, without question, some of our funniest moments.

Catharine Brandt (b. 1905)
American writer

Grandparents are people who play with children whether they are busy or not.

LANIE CARTER
20TH-CENTURY AMERICAN WRITER

*N*o cowboy was ever faster on a draw than a grandparent pulling a baby picture out of a wallet.

Anonymous

Mrs. Margaret Thatcher informed the world with regal panache yesterday that her daughter-in-law had given birth to a son. "We have become a grandmother," the Prime Minister said.

THE TIMES 4 MARCH 1989

When you look at your life,

the greatest happinesses are family happinesses.

Dr. Joyce Brothers (b. 1929)
American psychologist

If I am in a very confused situation in which I really need to make a decision, I always ask myself what my grandmother would do.

Isabel Allende (b. 1942)
Peruvian writer

It means you're a force in their lives who is too old to be shocked, too young to be out of it, too prejudiced to be unforgiving, too familiar with the parents to be on their side. . . .

Erma Bombeck (b. 1927)
American writer

You are the nonjudgmental adult
who lets them be themselves.
And who else can show them that life is
full of meaning—even after seventy?

ANNE MORROW LINDBERGH (B. 1906)
AMERICAN WRITER

A mother becomes a true grandmother the day she stops noticing the
terrible things her children do because she is so enchanted with the
wonderful things her grandchildren do.

Lois Wyse (b. 1926)
American writer

When the news came that Sevanne Margaret was born,

I suddenly realized that through no act of my own

I had become biologically related to a new human being.

This was the thing that had never come up in discussions of

grandparenthood and had never before occurred to me.

Margaret Mead (1901–1978)
American anthropologist

Our children are not going to be just "our children"—they are going to be other people's husbands and wives and the parents of our grandchildren.

Mary S. Calderone (b. 1904)
American medical lecturer and writer

I didn't expect this child to be such a source of affection. He doesn't give his grandmother one kiss, or even two kisses. Instead, his kisses are a rainforest where the rain never stops falling, little soft kisses in whichever bit of my face is nearest at that moment.

NELL DUNN (B. 1936)
ENGLISH WRITER

$\mathcal{A}$ strange feeling had gripped her as she looked down at the small dark head and tightly closed eyes, the tiny fists curled against the cheeks. This was not just another baby of millions being born every day, but a symbol of the continuity of life.

Nancy Cato (b. 1917)
Australian writer

What could be more beautiful than a dear old lady

growing wise with age?

Brigitte Bardot (b. 1933)
French actress

$\mathscr{G}$randma was a kind of first-aid station, or a Red Cross nurse, who took up where the battle ended, accepting us and our little sobbing sins, gathering the whole of us into her lap, restoring us to health and confidence by her amazing faith in life and in a mortal's strength to meet it.

Lillian Smith (1897–1966)
American writer, educator, and activist

My recommendation to any kid planning
to have a nice permissive childhood
is to have loving parents who come to
see him often, treat him with generosity
and affection, and leave him in the care
of an infatuated grandmother.

ED MCMAHON (B. 1923)
AMERICAN ENTERTAINER

Family faces are magic mirrors.
Looking at people who belong to us, we
see the past, present, and future.

Gail Lumet Buckley (b. 1937)
American writer

Grandparents are the family cement; the glue that keeps the extended family close, the reason sisters and brothers come to see one another on holidays or at special times.

Janet K. Balsky
20th-century American psychologist

*T*here is a certain melancholy in having to tell oneself that one has said good-bye — unless of course one is a grandmother — to the age and the circumstances that enable one to observe young children closely and passionately.

Colette [Sidonie-Gabrielle] (1873–1954)
French writer

One of the greatest contributions we can make to a grandchild's life is
to be the historians of family life as well as of the world in general.

EDA LESHAN (B. 1922)
AMERICAN WRITER

My grandmother, when she served dinner, was a virtuoso hanging on the edge of her own ecstatic performance. She seemed dissatisfied, almost querulous until she had corralled everybody into their chairs around the table, which she tried to do the minute they got into the house.

Patricia Hampl (b. 1946)
American writer

Although my grandmother lived out her long life in the shadow of Rainy Mountain, the immense landscape of the continental interior lay like a memory in her blood. She could tell of the Crows, whom she had never seen, and of the Black Hills, where she had never been.

N. Scott Momaday (b. 1934)
Native American (Kiowa) writer

Never have children, only grandchildren.

Gore Vidal (b. 1925)
American writer

This is what grandparenthood is all about. A happy, sweet-smelling baby whose college tuition you don't have to pay.

D. L. Stewart (b. 1942)
American columnist

orry a little bit every day and in a lifetime you will lose a couple of years. If something is wrong, fix it if you can. But train yourself not to worry. Worry never fixes anything.

MARY WELSH HEMINGWAY (1908–1986)
AMERICAN EDITOR AND WRITER

As a grandma you are a friend with a special power. You are a friend who can make toast. Better yet, you are a friend who can reach the cookie jar!

Leslie Lehr Spirson
20th-century American writer

A grandma's name is little less in love

Than is the doting title of a mother.

William Shakespeare (1564–1616)
English dramatist and poet

*A*n elderly lady who was asked by a child if she were young or old said: "My dear, I have been young a very long time."

ANONYMOUS

The old woman I shall become will be quite different from the
woman I am now. Another is beginning, and so far I have
not had to complain of her.

George Sand [Amandine Aurore Lucile Dupin] (1804–1876)
French writer

. . . old age is like a plane flying
through a storm. Once you're aboard,
there's nothing you can do. You can't
stop the plane, you can't stop the storm,
you can't stop time. So one might as
well accept it calmly, wisely.

GOLDA MEIR (1898–1978)
ISRAELI PRIME MINISTER

Grandmas are always slow but they do not mind
because they have all the time in the world.

Malcolm Andrew
20th-century American youth

Grandpa and Grandma might be old and decrepit, quiet, mellow, and unused to noise. They know a visit from the "grands" might do them in for a while, but they let you know every day they're thrilled you are there.

Alice Walker (b. 1944)
American writer

She delighted in being a grandmother. She had a horror of my leaving the children with a baby-sitter and thought nothing of taking the two-hour, three-bus trip to New Jersey to mind them.

Mary Higgins Clark (b. 1929)
American writer

Two daughters and a son, a trip to the ocean, an old car, grandchildren, all the things earned in a full and useful life.

TOM CLANCY (B. 1947)
AMERICAN WRITER

I look back on my life like a good day's work, it was done and I am satisfied with it. I was happy and contented. I knew nothing better and made the best out of what life offered. And life is what we make it, always has been, always will be.

Grandma [Anna Mary] Moses (1860–1961)
American artist

Becoming a grandparent fulfills the last stage of the life cycle,
enriching and crowning a lifetime's effort.

SIDNEY CALLAHAN
20TH-CENTURY AMERICAN PSYCHOLOGIST

Other things may change us, but we start and end with the family.

Anthony Brandt (b. 1936)
American writer